HAL LEONARD

DJEMBE METHOD

BY PAUL JENNINGS

To access video, visit:
www.halleonard.com/mylibrary

4628-2236-1152-0677

Notation by Alex Kosek

Photos by Natalie Champa Jennings

Bass player on videos: Scott Yonke

ISBN 978-1-4950-1986-9

HAL•LEONARD®
CORPORATION

7777 W. BLUEMOUND RD. P.O. BOX 13819 MILWAUKEE, WI 53213

Copyright © 2015 by HAL LEONARD CORPORATION
International Copyright Secured   All Rights Reserved

In Australia Contact:
Hal Leonard Australia Pty. Ltd.
4 Lentara Court
Cheltenham, Victoria, 3192 Australia
Email: ausadmin@halleonard.com.au

No part of this publication may be reproduced in any form or by
any means without the prior written permission of the Publisher.

Visit Hal Leonard Online at
www.halleonard.com

CONTENTS

PART 1: THE BASICS

ABOUT THE DJEMBE

The djembe is a goblet-shaped drum from West Africa that is widely believed to have had its origins with Mandinka black-smiths from the Mali Empire, known as the Numu. The Mali Empire dates to around 1230 C.E. and was made up of parts of modern-day countries including Mali, Senegal, Gambia, and Burkina Faso.

The djembe is traditionally used to accompany the rituals and dances of tribes in Senegal, Gambia, Mali, and other West African countries. Some of the tribal rhythms and musical pieces are quite complex and can be made up of several different layered djembe parts. These complex polyrhythmic patterns will usually include the use of other drums such as the dundun and the shekere.

The djembe is one of West Africa's most popular musical instruments and is most certainly one of the most popular hand percussion instruments in the world, with people using it in many musical genres.

ANATOMY OF THE DJEMBE

The body of the drum is usually carved from a single hardwood log. Traditionally, the skin of the djembe is goatskin; however, synthetic materials are becoming more commonly used. The traditional djembe is a rope-tuned drum with a complex pattern woven around the bowl of the djembe and pulled tight to increase tension on the skin.

With modern key-tuned djembes the skin is tuned by tightening or loosening tension rods that are evenly positioned around the bowl of the djembe. The tension rods are called lugs and are usually tightened with a drumkey or wrench.

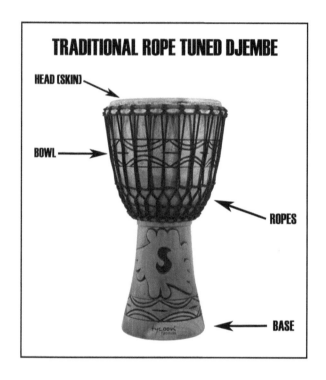

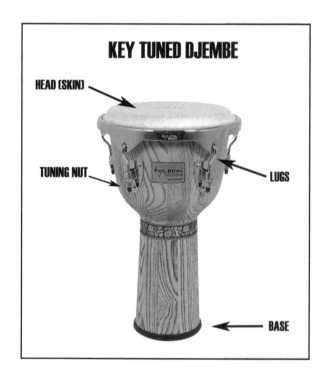

NOTATION KEY

Conventional music notation is written as notes on a staff. A staff has five lines with four spaces—one space between each line.

Five-line Staff

Barlines

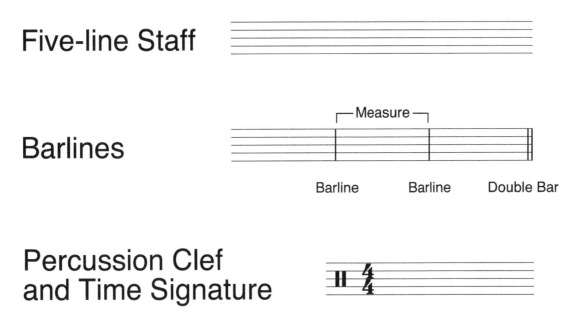

Barline   Barline   Double Bar

Percussion Clef and Time Signature

NOTATION SYMBOLS

The position of a note on the staff usually determines the pitch of the note. The notation used in this book for djembe is slightly different. The position of a note on the staff will determine which tone of the djembe is being used.

There are also different symbols for each tone of the djembe, which will make the notation easier to follow.

Djembe Notation Legend

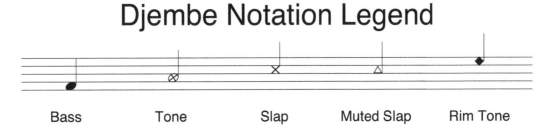

Bass   Tone   Slap   Muted Slap   Rim Tone

Other Musical Symbols

In this book other musical symbols are also used.

Accent: $>$
Accents are notes played with a greater emphasis. When a note has an accent symbol, you should play that note louder than the other notes.

Tie: $\smile$
A tie is a curved symbol that ties two notes together. You play the first note and sustain it through the value of the second note.

Hands:
The letters **R** and **L** tell you which hand to use for each note. **R** = Right hand, **L** = Left hand.

Important: All the lessons in this book are taught with a right-hand lead. If you are left-handed or feel more comfortable playing with a left-hand lead, feel free play the lessons that way.

READING NOTE VALUES

To be able to understand the lessons in this book, you will need to understand note values (how long each note lasts).

Each note symbol represents a different value. A whole note lasts for one whole bar (in 4/4 time), a half note's value is half of a whole note, a quarter note's value is a fourth of a whole note. We can keep subdividing all the way down to what are called sixty-fourth notes. The note value tree shown below subdivides the note values down to sixteenth notes.

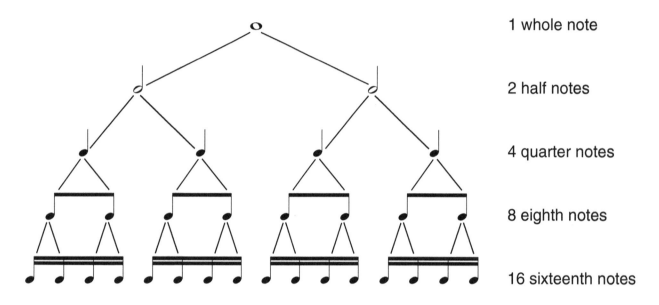

1 whole note

2 half notes

4 quarter notes

8 eighth notes

16 sixteenth notes

COUNTING

The majority of modern western music is notated and counted by dividing the rhythmic pulse into groups of four, meaning four separate beats. This is counted as: "1 2 3 4." These would be quarter notes.

You can then subdivide them into eighth notes: "1 and 2 and 3 and 4 and."

In this notation we will use the + symbol in place of the word "and": "1 + 2 + 3 + 4 +."

Sixteenth notes: "1 e + a 2 e + a 3 e + a 4 e + a."

When playing many of the grooves in this book that are in 4/4, It is very helpful to count out all the sixteenth notes in your head. This will help you figure out where each hit lands.

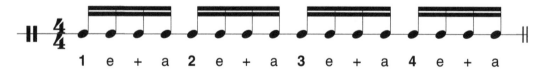

Triplets

Triplets are groups of three notes that are played in the space of two notes. The best way to count triplets is as follows:

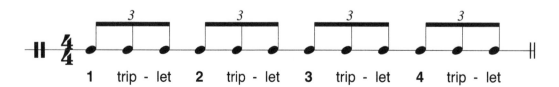

NOTE VALUE EXERCISES

These exercises will help you understand note values and get you familiar with reading the notation.

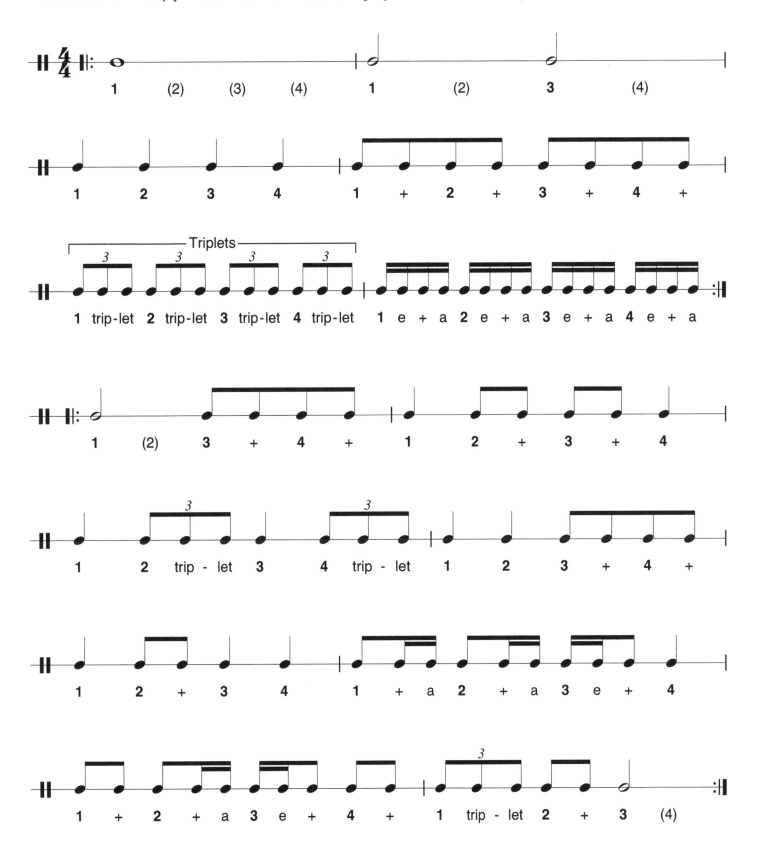

RESTS

A rest is a period of silence in music that is notated using a symbol that indicates the length or note value of the rest.

Whole Rest   Half Rest   Quarter Rest   Eighth Rest   16th Rest

Below are some rest exercises. When playing these exercises it is helpful to count out the note numbers and say "rest" when you should rest.

Rests Exercise

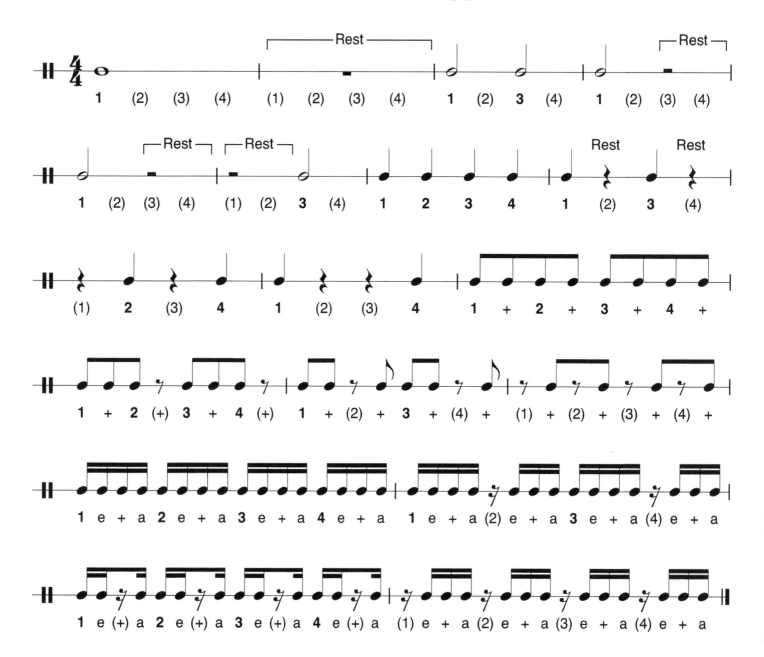

TUNING AND PLAYING POSITION

HOW SHOULD A DJEMBE BE TUNED?

Tuning a djembe is subjective, but most djembe players tune their drums to a fairly high pitch. This is to achieve a nice high slap while also getting a deep, resonant bass.

PLAYING POSITION

The djembe is played by striking the skin, located on the top of the drum, with your hands.

The djembe can be played while sitting down in a chair or on a stool, and it can also be played with the use of a harness or strap to allow the drummer to stand up while playing.

SITTING POSITION

When playing your djembe in a seated position you will need to use a stool or a chair with no arms.

The djembe should tilt forward and rest between your legs with your knees pressed against the sides to hold it in place. You should not have to use too much pressure. If your djembe is heavy, you may need to use a strap to help hold it in place. Bring your feet together so that the base of the djembe can rest there.

The skin should be roughly at your waist level so that you can play the drum easily. It is important to maintain a good, relaxed posture while playing.

STANDING POSITION

When playing while standing, make sure you have a harness or strap that can adequately support the weight of the djembe while you are playing it.

The djembe should rest between your legs with the skin roughly at your waist level so that you can play it easily.

BASS, TONE, AND SLAPS

BASS TONE

The bass is achieved by striking the djembe with a flat, relaxed hand in the center of the skin. Your hand should naturally bounce off the skin, allowing the bass tone to resonate. Keep your hands relaxed.

Follow this basic exercise for the bass tone. Hit the bass tone one time with each hand. Take it slowly at first. Count "1 2 3 4."

TONE

The tone is achieved by using a relaxed hand with your fingers closed. Make sure that your thumb is not hitting the djembe. Strike the djembe with the back of your knuckles (your palm) hitting the rim. Your fingers should naturally bounce off the skin with your fingers remaining closed.

Follow this basic exercise for the tone. Hit the tone four times with each hand. Take it slowly at first. Count "1 2 3 4."

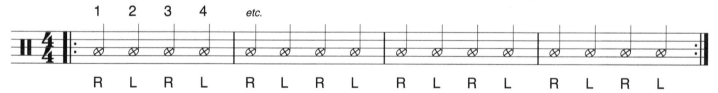

Tip:

• Play the exercises with a metronome set to a 4/4 pattern and start slowly (50 bpm or lower). Gradually increase the tempo as you get more comfortable with the exercise.

SLAP

The slap is the highest pitched tone of the djembe. You achieve the slap by allowing your fingers to be slightly open in a relaxed way. Bring your hands close to the rim. Slap the djembe so that your fingers bounce off the skin and create a loud, high slap. The back of your knuckles may also stay against the rim of your djembe while your fingers bounce off and create the slap.

Follow this basic exercise for the slap. Hit the slap one time with each hand. Take it nice and slow at first. Count "1 2 3 4."

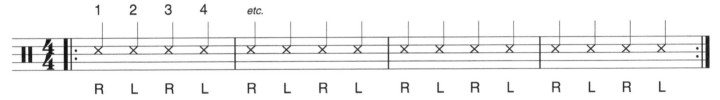

MUTED SLAP

The muted slap is a tone we will use later in the book, but it is important to learn it in the beginning. In a similar way to the slap tone, allow your fingers to be open in a relaxed way. This time you will be hitting the very edge of the djembe with the tips of your fingers, and you will have your other hand placed flat in the middle of the djembe to deaden the tone. Strive for a nice loud "pop" sound.

Follow this basic exercise for the muted slap. Hit the muted slap one time with each hand. Alternate which hand is acting as the mute and which is the striking hand. Count "1 2 3 4."

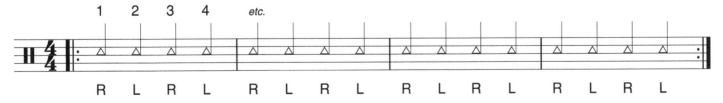

Tip:

• It may take some time and practice to get good tones. Be patient, practice regularly, and you will have the tones down in no time.

THREE TONE EXERCISE

 You have now learned the four tones of the djembe, and you are ready to move onto some exercises and patterns.

In this simple exercise you will practice alternating between the bass, tone, and slap. The exercise will help you become more comfortable playing the three main tones as well as introducing you to playing a basic rhythm on the djembe.

Focus on your tone and make sure you are getting a nice solid bass, a resonant tone, and good crack for the slap.

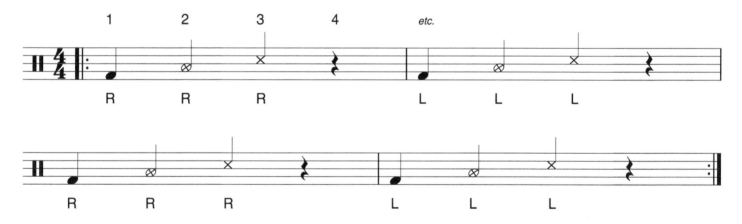

Repeat the pattern and try to keep it going as long as you can.

Tips:

- Use a metronome to help you keep a good tempo and build a solid sense of timing.

- Start slow! It can take your muscle memory many repetitions to get comfortable with the pattern. Gradually increase the tempo.

- Maintain good posture.

TONE AND MUTED SLAP EXERCISES

 Now we will play an exercise using the tone and muted slap. This will not only help your tone get better but also help you get familiar with placing the muted slap in a pattern.

We are playing three hits on the tone with the right hand, followed by a muted slap also played on the right hand (with the left hand as the mute). Follow the same with our left hand.

Pay close attention to when you slide your left hand into the middle of the djembe to mute the slap. The timing of this move is important and will eventually feel natural.

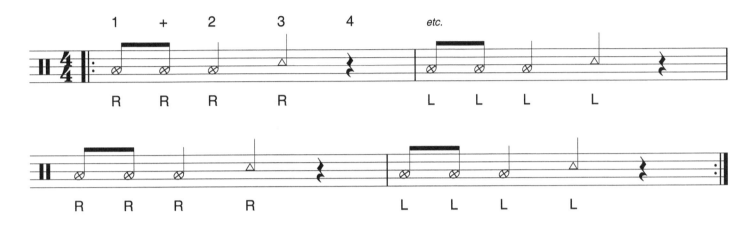

Now let's try bringing in the bass.

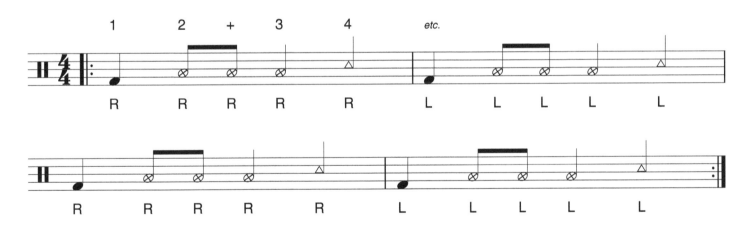

Repeat the pattern and try to keep it going as long as you can.

Tips:

- Pay attention to the timing of when you slide your hand into the middle for the muted slap.

- Remember to keep your fingers closed for the tone.

- Remember to let your hand bounce off the skin for the bass tone.

- Your fingers should be open and relaxed for the slap tone.

THREE TONE DOUBLE EXERCISES

 Now we will introduce playing doubles, which means we will play two hits with one hand before moving to the other hand.

Start by playing two bass notes with your right hand, then two bass notes with your left. Do the same with the tone and slap, and repeat.

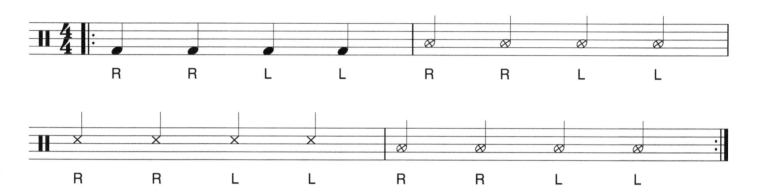

VARIATION

This is a variation using only the bass and tone.

Play two bass notes using your right hand, then play two tone notes using your left hand. Then play two tones with your right hand followed by two bass notes with your left hand.

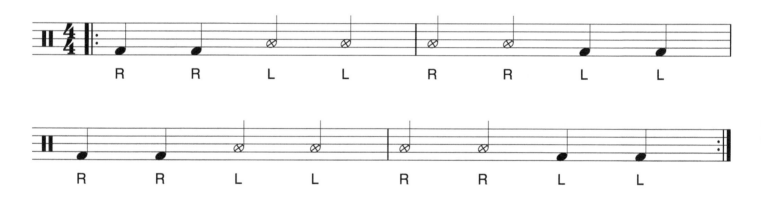

Try to keep the exercises going, play the beats evenly spaced and with the same force.

Tips:

- Always check that you are playing each tone correctly.

- If your hands get sore, take a break.

BASIC 4/4 RHYTHM

 Now that you have learned the four basic tones of the djembe and worked on some exercises, it is time to learn your first rhythm.

This rhythm is in 4/4, so there are four beats in each bar.

We are going to count the groove like this: **1** e + a **2** e + a **3** e + a **4** e + a

WHERE THE HITS LAND

The groove begins on beat 1 of the bar with a bass tone hit by the right hand. The next hit is a tone with the left hand, which lands on the "a" just before beat 2. The next hit lands with the right hand on beat 2. The next beat is on the "+" with a left-hand tone. The next hit is a slap with the right hand on beat 3. The next is a tone with the left hand on the "a" just before beat 4. The next is a right-hand tone on beat 4. The final hit is a left-hand tone on the "+" before the next bar.

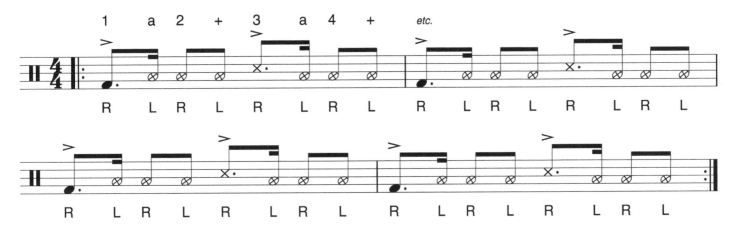

Well done! You are playing your first djembe rhythm.

BASIC 4/4 RHYTHM VARIATION

Here is a variation of the basic 4/4 rhythm.

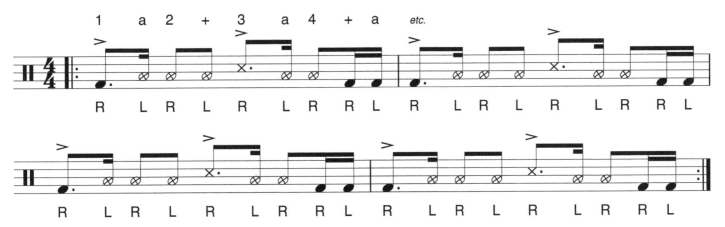

Tips:

- Practice this rhythm with a metronome. Use a slower bpm at first, then increase the tempo as you feel comfortable.

- Take it slow and don't get frustrated. With some good, solid practice you will have this groove down in no time.

WEST AFRICAN DJEMBE RHYTHMS

West African rhythms were traditionally created to accompany dances and rituals. They are typically made up of several parts played on djembe as well as other drums. These interlocking parts make up the piece, and even though it is fine to play each rhythm on its own, nothing beats getting together with other drummers and playing the parts together.

THE BREAK

 Most West African rhythms begin and end with what is called a "break." The break is just a simple line that signals the beginning and end of a piece. It can also signal a transition in the piece of music being played.

This is a universal break that is used with many 4/4 rhythms. You will see this break used with many of the rhythms in this book.

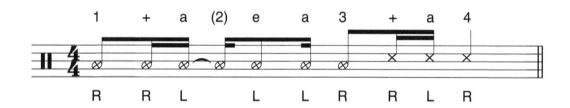

KUKU

Kuku is one of the most popular West African rhythms. Its origins are with the Manian people of the forest region of Guinea. Kuku was originally used for women to dance to when returning from fishing and is now used for many types of celebrations. It can vary in speeds depending on the region.

KUKU PART 1

These are the second and third djembe parts of the Kuku rhythm. If you are playing with one or more other djembe players, you can each take one of these parts and play them simultaneously.

Also practice using the 4/4 break at the beginning and end of your drumming session.

KUKU PART 2

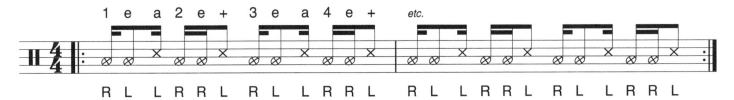

KUKU PART 3

Tips:

- This rhythm is counted in 4/4 time.

- You can use a metronome while playing to keep you in the right place.

- If you can find a friend or two to play with, try playing the different parts together.

GHOST NOTES

 Ghost notes so named because they are quiet and sometimes barely there. We use them to give a groove some character and flavor in between the main, accented beats.

Ghost note symbol:

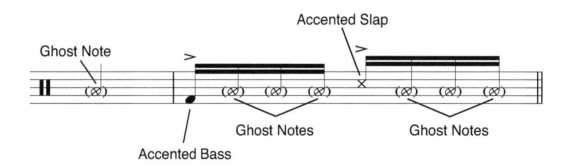

Whenever you see the ghost note symbol, play that note very softly.

GHOST NOTE EXERCISE

In this ghost note exercise we are going to play all of the sixteenth notes as ghost notes with tone hits and play the bass and slap hits as the main, accented beats.

Be aware of the volume of the ghost notes compared to the main beats. There should be a clear difference in volume, with the main beats at a normal volume and the ghost notes much softer.

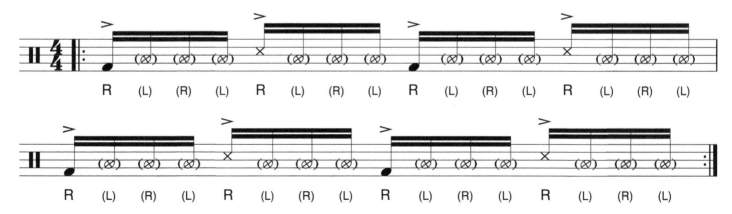

THE FLAM

The flam is a basic stroke that is used alongside the single stroke. Its main purpose is to create a longer sounding note. The flam is comprised of two single hits that are played at different velocities. The loudest hit is sometimes called the primary note. The softer hit is called a grace note. The grace note should be played just before the primary note.

The grace note is not supposed to have a rhythmic value. This is because a flam can have a different feel depending on how far apart you play each note.

It can take time to be able to play a good flam. You should practice playing flams with the grace note as close as you can get it to the primary note and also at a further distance.

Also note that the grace note and primary note are attached to each other with a tie: ⌣

FLAM EXERCISES

Left-Hand Lead

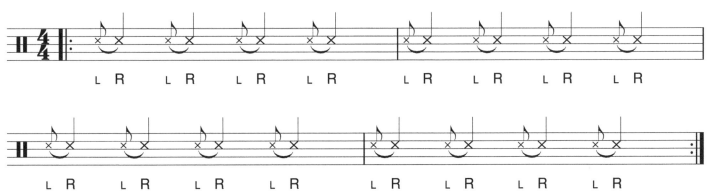

Right-Hand Lead

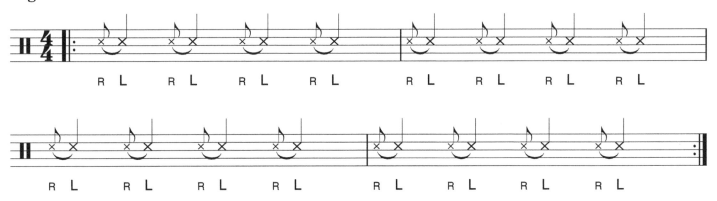

BASIC 6/8 RHYTHM

These rhythms are in 6/8 time, so there are six beats in each bar counted as eighth notes.

Let's try the 6/8 rhythm first with no ghost notes.

Now let's play the same rhythm and introduce the ghost notes.

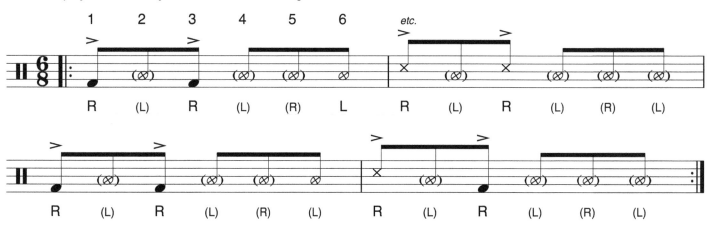

BASIC 6/8 RHYTHM VARIATION

Here is a variation of the basic 6/8 rhythm. This one has ghost notes.

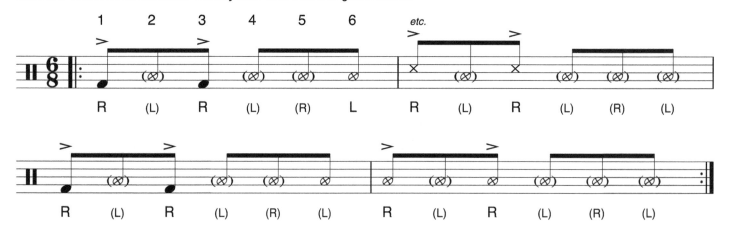

Tip:

- Set a metronome to 6/8 time to practice this rhythm. Use a slower bpm at first, then increase the tempo as you feel comfortable.

PART 2: TRADITIONAL DJEMBE RHYTHMS

LAMBAN

The Lamban is a rhythm played in honor of West African storytellers and historians known as griots. Traditionally the Lamban was not played on djembe but on other instruments such as the talking drum and balafon. The Lamban can also be known as the Lamba, Sandia, or Djelidon.

BREAK

LAMBAN PART 1

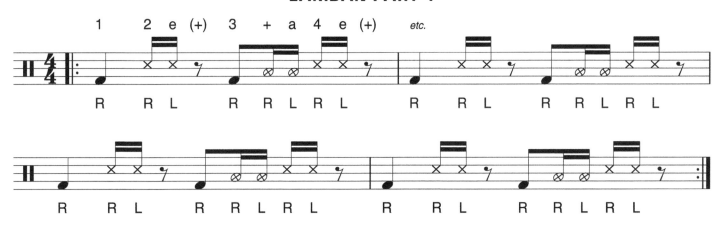

LAMBAN PART 2

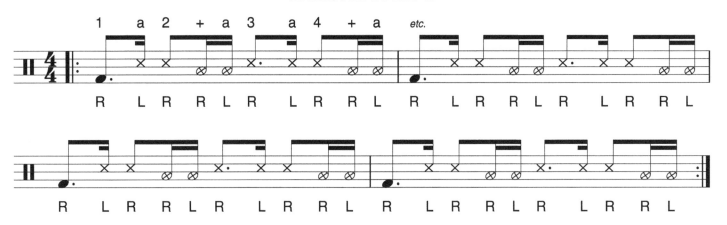

DUNUNBA (DONABA)

 Dununba means "strong man's dance." This rhythm usually accompanies a dance, which was a sometimes violent fight between the men to establish superiority in the village.

There are many forms of Dununba; this one is called "Donaba."

TIME SIGNATURE

Donaba is counted in 12/8, meaning there are twelve eighth notes in each bar.

DONABA PART 1

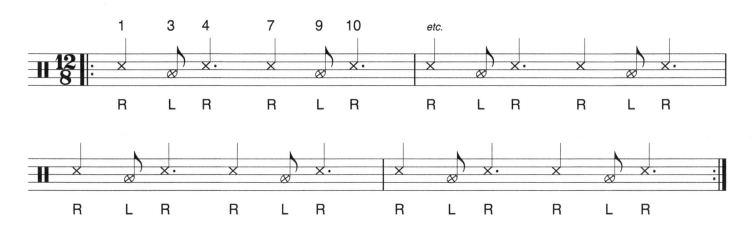

DONABA PART 2

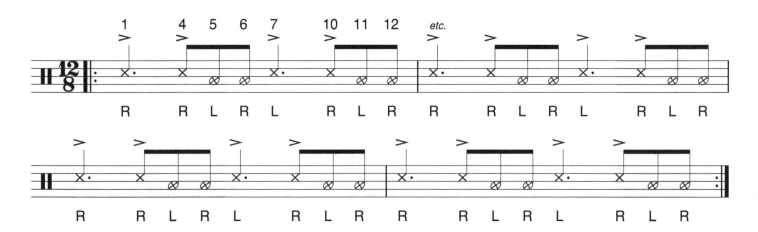

DJOLÉ

Djolé is a famous West African rhythm played all across the region. Traditionally Djolé was a mask dance in which a man wore a mask depicting a woman. Djolé was usually a big festivity where villages came together to celebrate occasions like the end of harvest.

BREAK

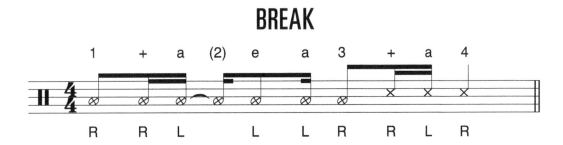

DJOLÉ PART 1

DJOLÉ PART 2

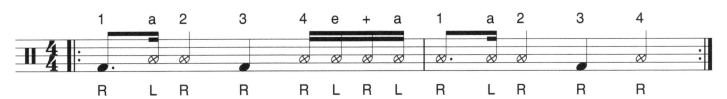

DJOLÉ PART 3

DENADON

The Denadon rhythm is traditionally played as a welcome dance before festivals.

BREAK

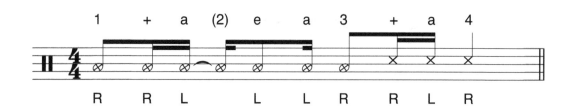

DENADON PART 1

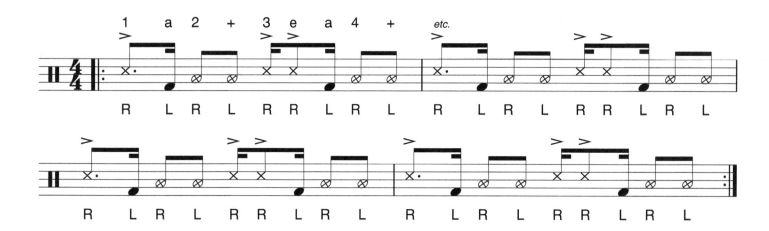

DENADON PART 2

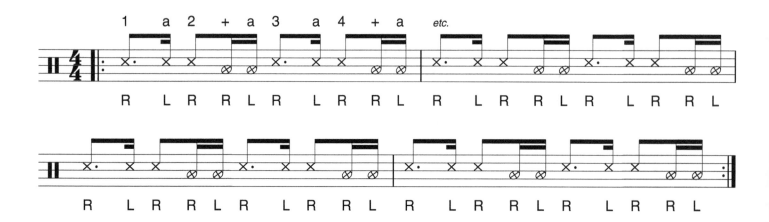

N'GORON

This rhythm originated with the Senufo tribe of Ivory Coast. Traditionaly, N'Goron was played after the initiation of the girls of the tribe.

BREAK

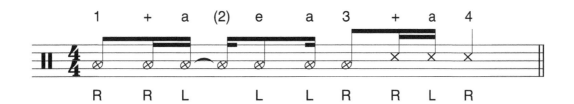

N'GORON PART 1

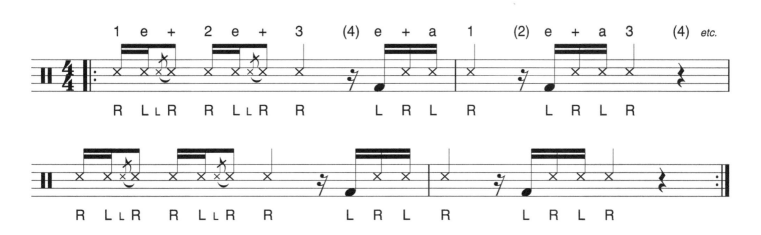

N'GORON PART 2

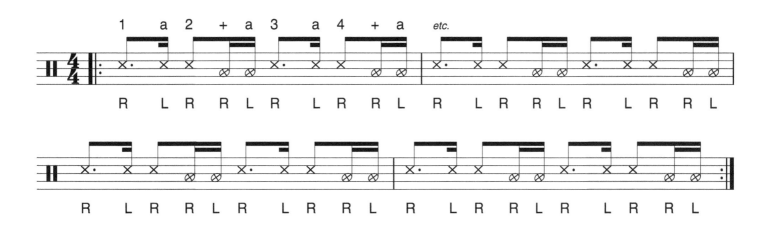

SOKO

 Soko was traditionally a rhythm played as children traveled from village to village to notify their relatives of circumcision rituals.

SOKO BREAK

SOKO PART 1

SOKO PART 2

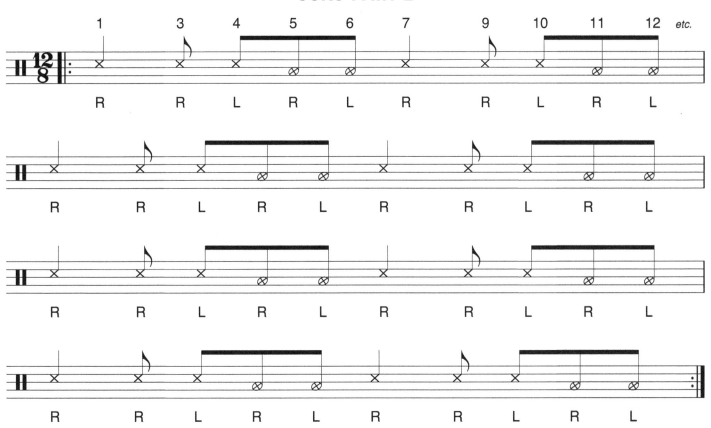

SOKO PART 3

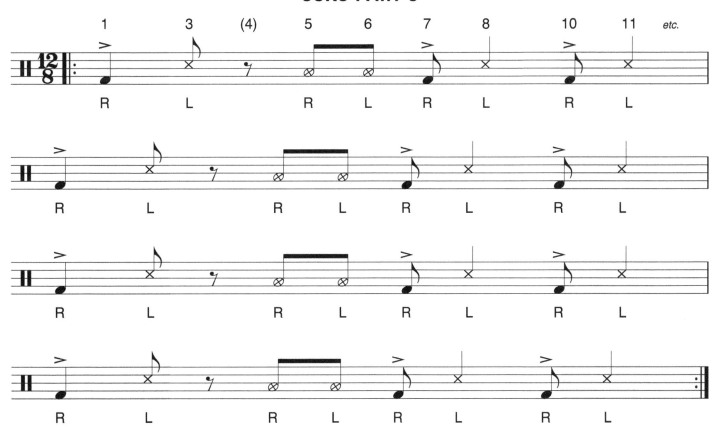

KASSA

 Kassa was traditionally a harvest dance and played to help support the workers in the fields tending to their crops.

BREAK

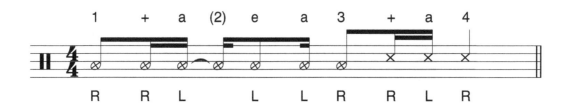

KASSA PART 1

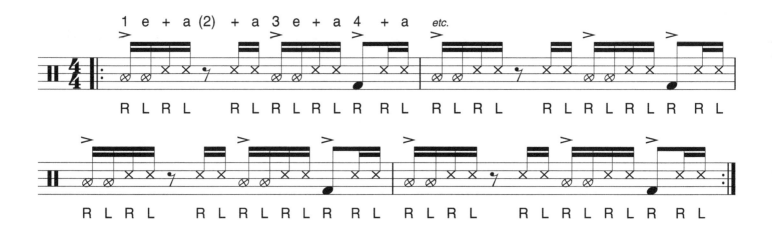

KASSA PART 2

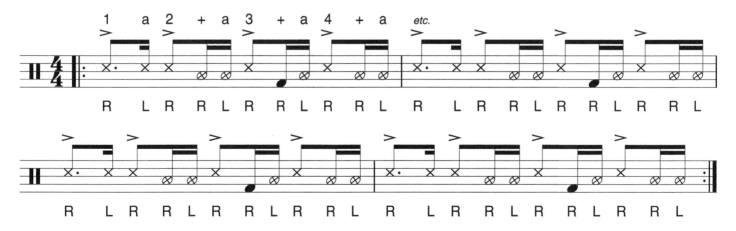

SOFA

The word "Sofa" translates as "warrior." The Sofa rhythm was used to celebrate the warriors of the village and bring them luck and victory.

BREAK

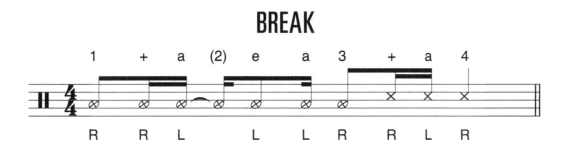

SOFA PART 1

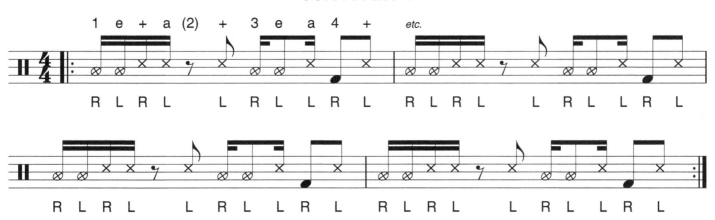

SOFA PART 2

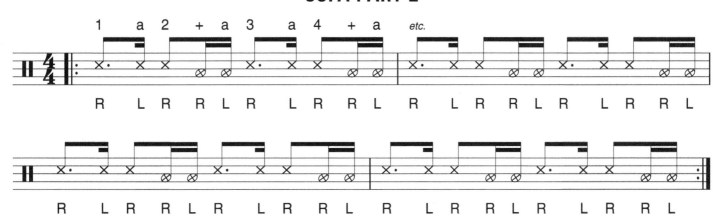

PART 3: MODERN TECHNIQUE

Although the djembe is traditionally a West African instrument and it has a huge amount of traditional rhythms, which I encourage you to explore, many players are also using the instrument for other genres of music.

In this chapter we will explore modern rhythms such as rock, funk, and blues, as well as some rhythms from Latin America and the Middle East.

ROCK

 We are going to start with rock because that genre is familiar to most of us and also works great on the djembe.

ROCK 1

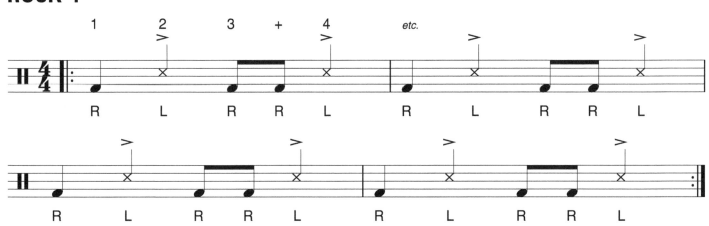

ROCK 2

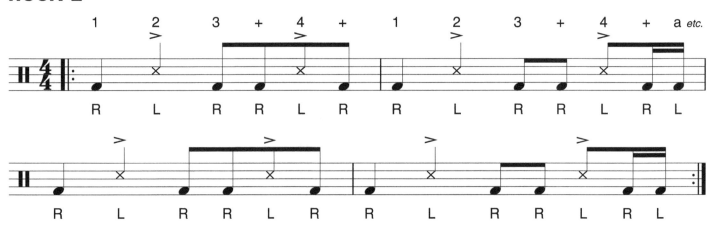

ROCK 3

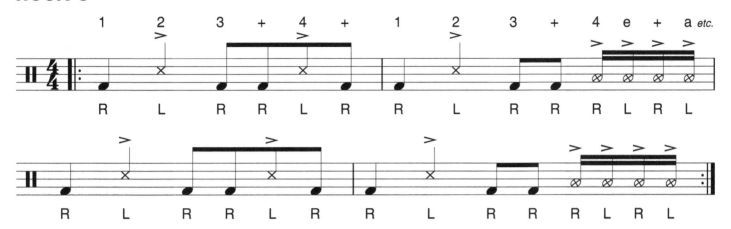

Tips:

- Try playing along with a favorite rock song using one of the rock rhythms.

- Try playing the rock rhythms in a sequence together.

RIM TONE

 The rim tone can be used in many grooves and also is great for use in solos. It is called the rim tone because we literally strike the rim of the djembe to achieve it.

The rim tone is achieved by striking the edge of the djembe with the tips of your fingers.

RIM TONE EXERCISE

Practice this exercise to get familiar with playing the rim tone. Note where the rim tone is placed on the staff and the symbol that is used for it.

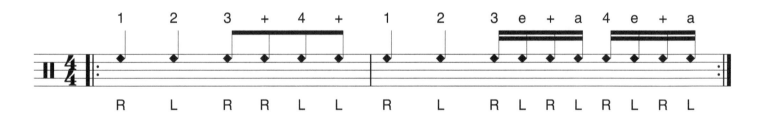

Tips:

- For fun, try incorporating the rim tone in other rhythms of this book.

- If your fingers get sore, take a break

REGGAE

 Many people will be familiar with reggae, which was largely popularized in the 20th century by such artists as Bob Marley. The tone of the djembe suits reggae very well.

Reggae has a distinctive rhythmic feel. Unlike conventional 4/4 rhythms such as rock, there is usually no bass hit on beat 1 of the bar. There is also usually a strong hi-hat pattern, which we'll play with the rim tone on the djembe.

REGGAE 1

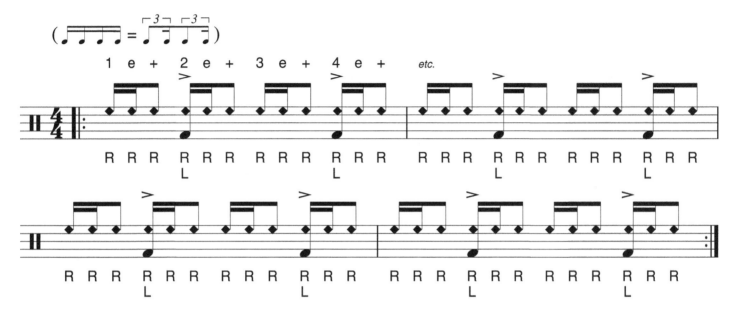

REGGAE 2

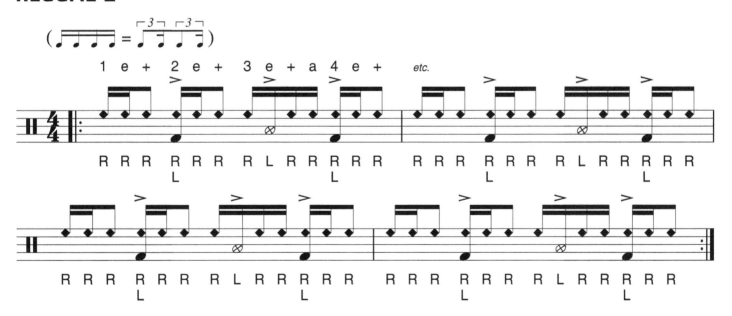

Tips:

- Find a reggae track to play along with.

- Listen for the distinctive feel and try to match it.

BLUES SHUFFLE

 The blues shuffle is in 12/8, which can be counted with a "four feel": "1 + a 2 + a 3 + a 4 + a."

BLUES SHUFFLE 1

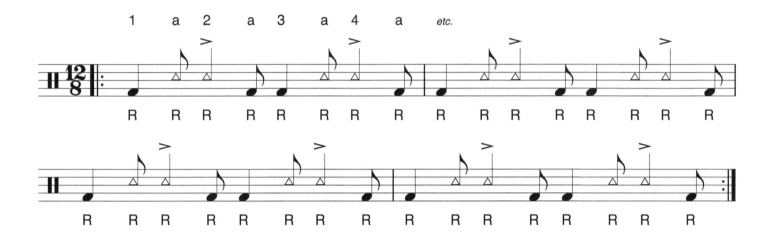

BLUES SHUFFLE 2

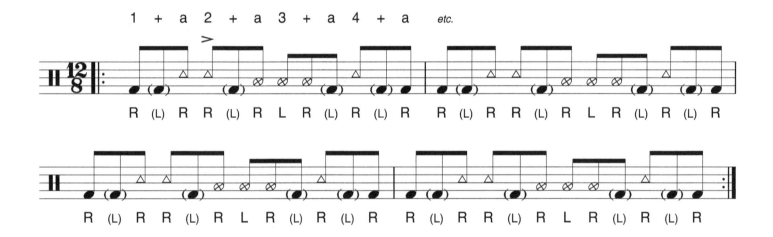

Tips:

- These blues shuffles are notated in 12/8. They have a distinctive shuffle feel.

- You don't need to only use these rhythms with blues. If the rhythm fits with another 12/8 song or piece, use it.

FUNK

 Funk sometimes sounds a lot like rock, although the feel of the groove is different. Funk is typically focused on an on-beat/off-beat structure. Usually a greater emphasis is placed on the first beat of the bar and a solid back-beat is played on the snare (slap) hits.

FUNK 1

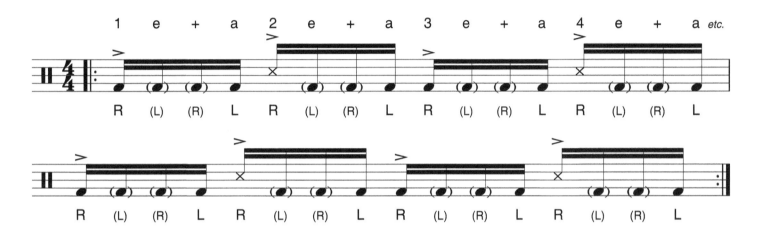

FUNK 2

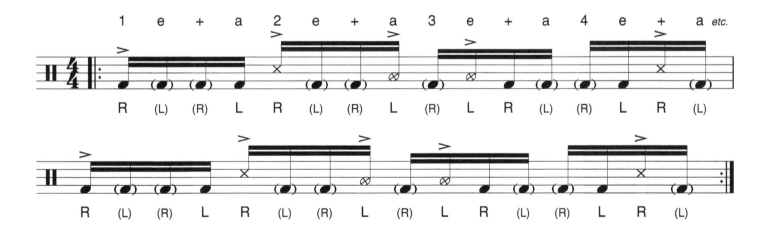

Tip:

• Pay attention to the distinctive feel and rhythmic accents of funk.

HIP-HOP

 The hip-hop style is similar to funk, and you could also play these rhythms in a funk song. These rhythms work pretty nicely on the djembe.

HIP-HOP 1

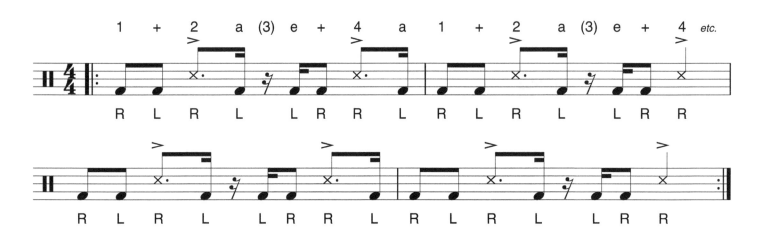

HIP-HOP 2

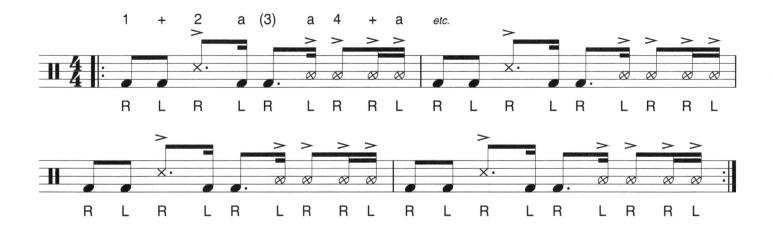

PALM ROLLING

The palm rolling technique is typically used with congas, but it can also be applied to many other drums.

The technique is used to play fast rudiments including rolls on hand drums, but is also used for slower techniques and ghost notes.

In this book we will be using it to play ghost notes in the Guaguancó and Salsa rhythms.

We will use the following symbols to notate when the palm rolling technique is used:

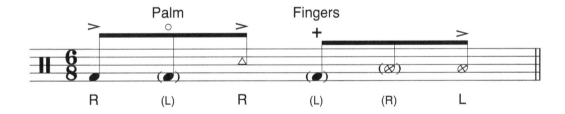

Tips:

- Try to play a "heel/toe" motion with your palm and fingertips on the drum: one palm-down note, then one fingertips-down note on each hand.

- Try to keep it uniform and sounding the same with each hand.

SALSA

 Salsa is one of the most common rhythms played in Latin American music. This Salsa rhythm is usually played on congas but can also be adapted to djembe.

This is notated in what is called "cut-time." This means that the bar is cut in two, so a bar of 4/4 would become a bar of 2/2. Salsa is usually played at a fast tempo, so cut-time is used to make the notation easier to read at a faster tempo.

Also note the "pickup" notes at the beginning of the bar with the salsa rhythms and the use of the palm rolling technique for some of the ghost notes.

SALSA 1

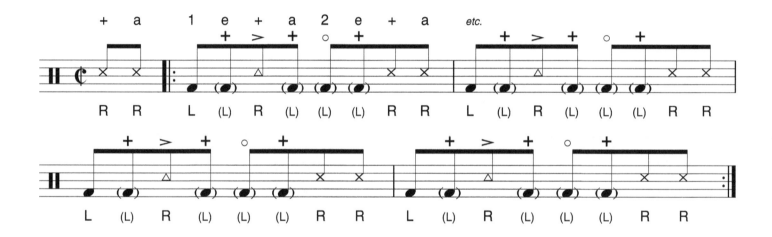

SALSA 2

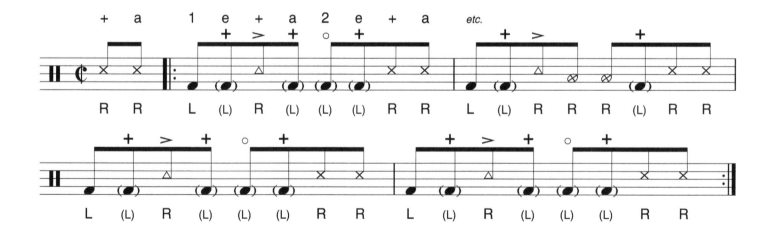

Tip:

• Listen to some salsa music and try playing along. Listen to how the salsa rhythm works in with the music.

MIDDLE EASTERN

 This is a Middle Eastern rhythm that can be heard across many traditions throughout the region.

MIDDLE EASTERN 1

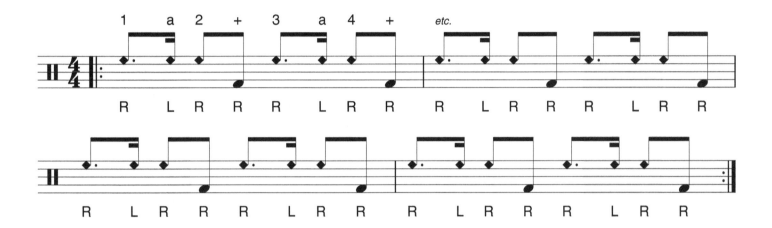

MIDDLE EASTERN 2

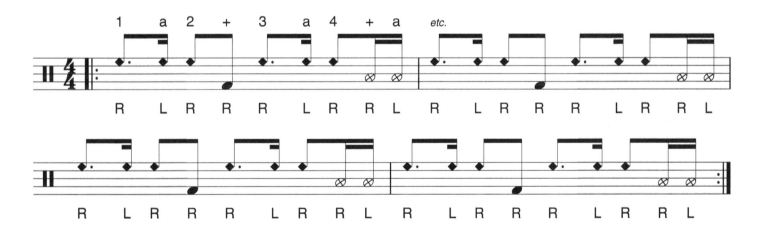

GUAGUANCÓ

Guaguancó is a form of Cuban Rumba, which usually combines congas, other percussion, vocals, and dance.

You will notice that this Guaguancó rhythm is in 4/4 and has two notes before the bar begins on beat 1. These are called "pickup notes" and are notated to indicate that the rhythm begins before beat 1 of the bar.

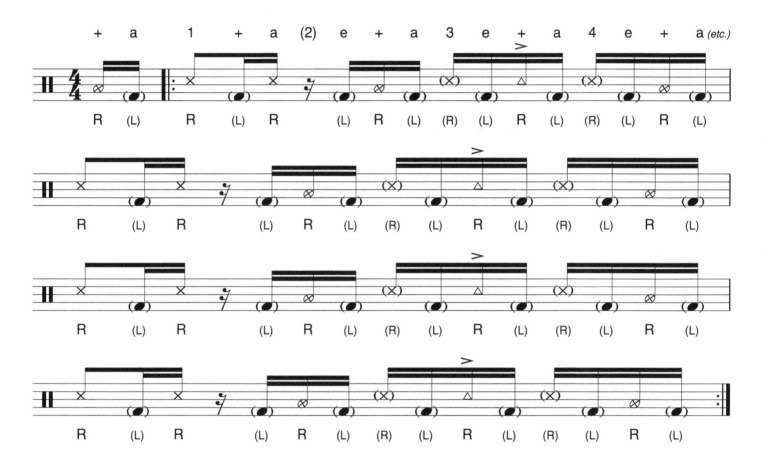

Tip:

• Find a Guaguancó track and try playing along. YouTube™ is a great place to find examples of rhythms like this.

SAMBA

 Samba is a type of music from Brazil. Samba has its roots in Africa and is recognized worldwide as a symbol of Brazilian culture.

CUT-TIME

Samba is traditionally notated in "cut-time." This means that the bar is cut in two, so a bar of 4/4 becomes a bar of 2/2. Samba is usually played at a fast tempo, so cut-time is used to make the notation easier to read at a faster tempo.

SAMBA

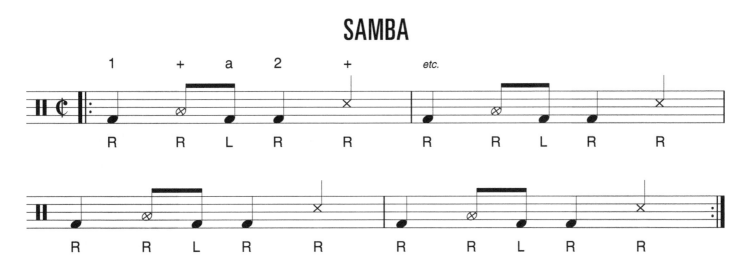

MOZAMBIQUE

 Mozambique is a type of music from Cuba, particularly the Afro-Cuban tradition.

Pay particular attention to the ride cymbal pattern, which we play as a rim tone on the djembe. Also remember that when two notes are tied, you do not play the second note.

MOZAMBIQUE

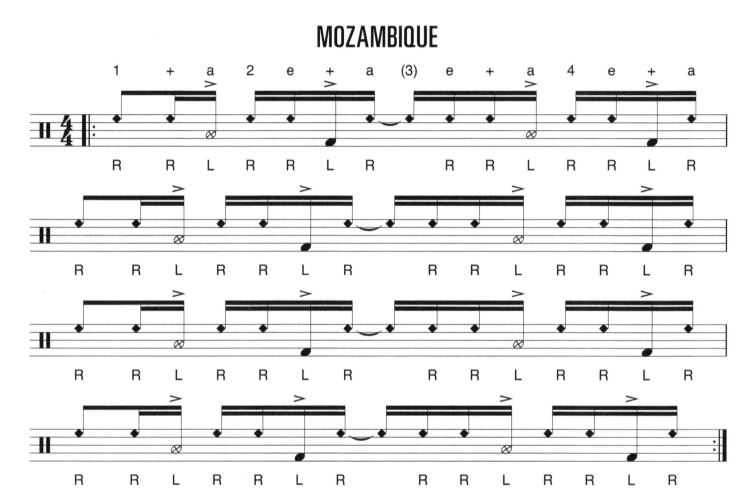

RUMBA

 Rumba can be found in many musical traditions, particularly in Latin America, and it is widely used in the Afro-Cuban tradition.

RUMBA 1

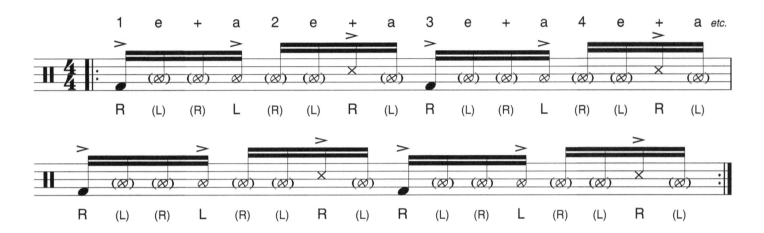

RUMBA 2

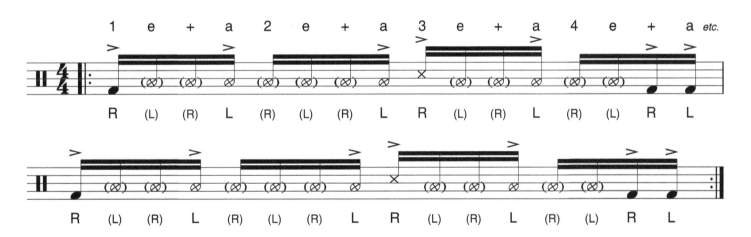

12/8 FUNK

This is a 12/8 funk rhythm that has a heavy use of ghost notes.

MUTED 12/8 RHYTHM

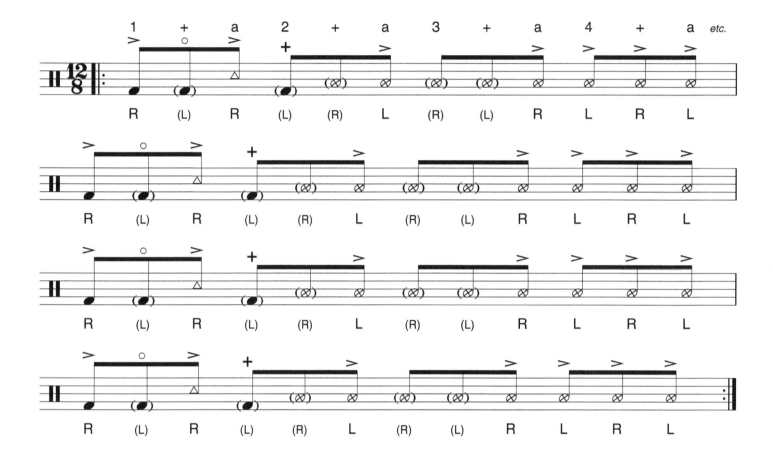

PARADIDDLE

The paradiddle is one of the most common drumming rudiments and can also be effective when used on the djembe.

The hand pattern is **RLRR LRLL**, and the pattern repeats.

BASS PARADIDDLE

BASS AND TONE PARADIDDLE

HAND SWITCH PARADIDDLE

DJEMBE FINALE

BY PAUL JENNINGS

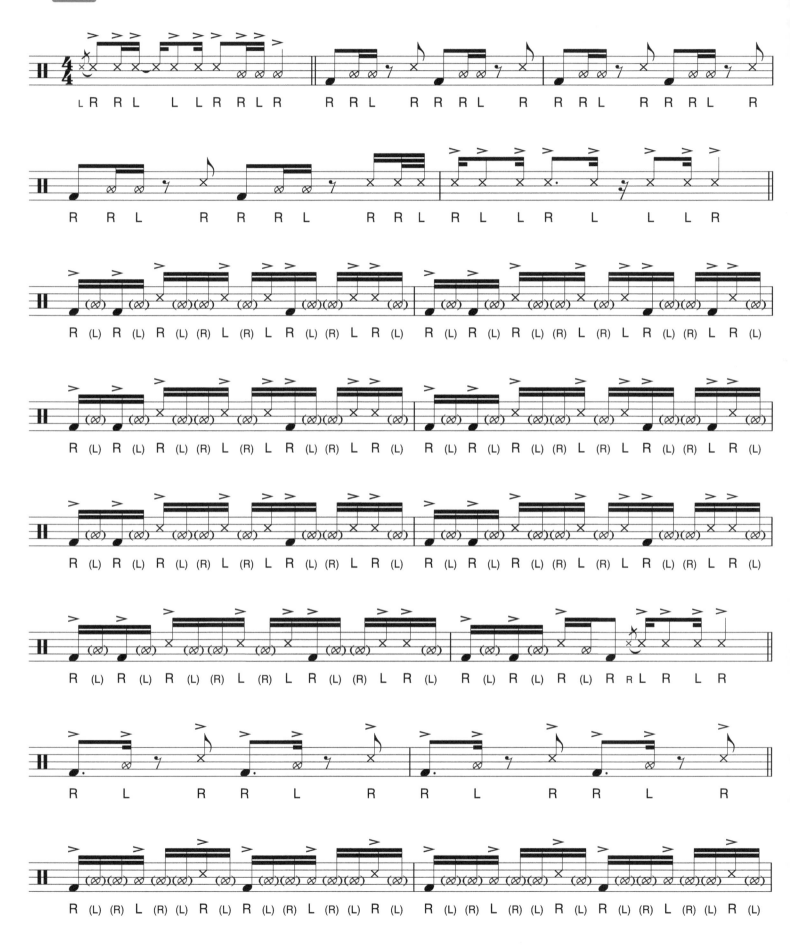

Congratulations! You have now completed the *Hal Leonard Djembe Method* book. You should feel very proud of yourself. You are now playing at an intermediate level and ready to take your playing even further.

HAL LEONARD DRUM & PERCUSSION METHODS

HAL LEONARD HAL LEONARD CAJON METHOD
by Paul Jennings

This beginner's guide for anyone learning to play the cajon takes you through the basics of the instrument and its techniques with dozens of exercises and over 30 grooves from many genres including rock, Latin, blues, jazz, flamenco, funk, and more. There are also more advanced techniques in the final chapter that include how to change the pitch with your foot, playing with brushes, and playing rolls with your fingers.

00138215 Book/Online Video $12.99

HAL LEONARD HANDPAN METHOD
by Mark D'Ambrosio & Jenny Robinson

The *Hal Leonard Handpan Method* is written for a broad range of skill levels. Beginners will find the introductory material and exercises necessary to develop their touch and technical skill, while the advanced player will find instructions on how to execute high-level techniques, create sophisticated sounds, and build complex patterns. The information, techniques, and theory presented in this book are designed to be flexible, and can be adapted to work on your instrument, no matter the scale or number of notes. The price of this book includes access to videos online, for download or streaming, using the unique code included with each purchase.

00288061 Book/Online Video $14.99

HAL LEONARD DJEMBE METHOD
by Paul Jennings

This beginner's guide takes you through the basics of the instrument and its techniques. The accompanying online videos include demonstrations of many examples in the book. Topics covered include: notation • bass and slap tone exercises • three- and four-tone exercises • basic rhythms • traditional djembe rhythms • modern techniques • and much more.

00145559 Book/Online Video $14.99

HAL LEONARD SNARE DRUM METHOD
by Rick Mattingly

Geared toward beginning band and orchestra students, this modern, musical approach to learning snare drum includes play-along audio files that feature full concert band recordings of band arrangements and classic marches with complete drum parts that allow the beginning drummer to apply the book's lessons in a realistic way.

06620059 Book/Online Audio...........................$10.99

HAL LEONARD DRUMSET METHOD
by Kennan Wylie with Gregg Bissonette

Lessons in Book 1 include: drum setup & fundamentals • tuning & maintenance • basic music reading • grips & strokes • coordination & basic techniques • basic beats for many styles of music • 8th notes, 16th notes, dotted notes & triplets • drum fills • and more. Lessons in Book 2 include: limb independence • half-time grooves • syncopation • funk grooves • ghost notes • jazz drumming • chart reading • drum soloing • brush playing • and much more.

00209864 Book 1/Online Media.......................$17.99
00209865 Book 2/Online Media.......................$16.99
00209866 Books 1 & 2/
          Online Media, Comb-Bound............$27.50

HAL LEONARD STEELPAN METHOD
by Liam Teague

The *Hal Leonard Steelpan Method* is designed for anyone just learning to play the steelpan. This easy-to-use beginner's guide takes you through the basics of the instrument and its technique. It covers: stance • holding the mallets • types of strokes • tone production and volume control • stickings • rolls • scales • calypsos • many songs and exercises • basic music reading • steelpan anatomy and maintenance • steelpan history • and more.

00111629 Book/Online Audio...........................$12.99

HAL LEONARD DRUMS FOR KIDS

Drums for Kids is a fun, easy course that teaches children to play drumset faster than ever before. Popular songs will keep kids motivated, while the simple, easy-to-read page layouts ensure their attention remains focused on one concept at a time. The method can be used in combination with a drum teacher or parent.

00113420 Book/Online Audio...........................$12.99

See these and many other percussion titles at
halleonard.com

Order today from your favorite music retailer at **halleonard.com**
Prices, contents and availability subject to change without notice.